P9-EMN-439

Positive Performance Management:

A Guide to

"*Win-* Date Due *ws*

Written by John Mattone
Edited by National Press Publications

NATIONAL PRESS PUBLICATIONS
A Division of Rockhurst College Continuing Education Center, Inc.
6901 West 63rd Street • P.O. Box 2949 • Shawnee Mission, Kansas 66201-1349
1-800-258-7246 • 1-913-432-7757

Positive Performance Management
A Guide to "Win-Win" Reviews
© 1988 National Press Publications
A Division of Rockhurst College Continuing Education Center, Inc.

Printed in the United States of America

8   9   10

ISBN 1-55852-003-1

Table of Contents

1

APPRAISALS:
COMPLETE, HONEST, TIMELY

The fundamental belief underlying Positive Performance Management is this: Managers and employees must strive to make performance appraisals complete, honest and timely.

As a manager, you need to make sure that each employee knows where he or she stands at all times in the organization. When telling someone how they rate, you as a manager must be fair and honest, never injuring a person's sense of dignity. Further, you must give employees the opportunity to make certain career decisions on what is best for them.

Just as employees need to know where they stand, the organization needs to know where it stands with respect to its employees. It is entitled to a fair and honest appraisal. This will help the organization make the best moves in regard to promotion, transfer, discipline or termination.

This strategy pays off handsomely in such things as increased sales, profits or productivity for the organization.

What if the Truth Isn't Told?

If you tell an employee, intentionally, that he is doing *worse* than he is, you may cause many problems.

Untruthful poor appraisals can cause:

- Dissatisfaction. ("They don't understand me no matter what I say or do.")

- Reduced motivation. ("Why try? My boss doesn't appreciate what I do.")

- Reduced commitment. ("This company doesn't care about me. Why should I care about it?")

- Voluntary, or even involuntary, termination of employment. ("Enough is enough. I'll go where I am understood.")

Thus, if you say a person's work is worse than it is, the organization runs the risk of losing a person who, may be valuable.

What if you intentionally over-praise someone, assess their work as better than it is?

Untruthful good appraisals can cause:

- Coasting. ("My boss told me I was doing great, so I'll just cruise along with my usual half effort.")

- Complaints of unfairness. ("You give me static for my performance, but he does worse and you praise him.")

- Problems in disciplining or terminating the employee later. ("What? Poor work? You told me last year right in this office I was doing real good work.")

Clearly, beyond the ethical considerations, there are practical, legal and administrative reasons for giving an employee a straight, honest evaluation.

2

WHAT ARE THE TEN ELEMENTS OF POSITIVE PERFORMANCE MANAGEMENT ?

Listed here are the critical elements of Positive Performance Management, the elements that lead to "win-win" appraisals. They will be discussed in detail in subsequent sections. They are presented here in outline form to help put the whole process in perspective.

1. *Employee involvement* — You should set objectives with employee input.

2. *Valid performance criteria* — You should rate employees only on those criteria/factors that determine success in their position.

3. *Year-round process* — Your employees are entitled to feedback throughout the year.

4. ***Proper preparation*** — Managers *and* employees need to spend time preparing for appraisals.

5. ***Avoid stereotypical thinking*** — As a manager, you need to block biases out when rating your employees. Evaluate their work and contributions to the organization.

6. ***Input from others*** — Managers need to get performance appraisal input from others (if they can provide valid performance data regarding the employee.)

7. ***Consistency*** — You need to send a clear, consistent message. Don't let your words say one thing while your manner says another.

8. ***Transition*** — The final rating is based on *what* was accomplished and how it was accomplished.

9. ***Dialogue*** — Between manager and employee is critical throughout the year.

10. ***Employee ownership*** — It is the employee's name and rating which appears on the appraisal form. His pay increases are determined by the rating as well as his promotional opportunities. Therefore, it is the *employee's* appraisal and not necessarily management's. Because this is so, employees should be entitled to a much larger role in shaping their own appraisal.

3

THE THREE-PART CYCLE

Positive Performance Management has three phases that repeat:

1. Performance Appraisal/Goal-Setting

2. Coaching

3. Reviewing Performance Goals

These three phases include the following:

1. Performance Appraisal/Goal-Setting represents the typical once-a-year meeting between the manager and employee. All employees should receive an annual appraisal.

- *Performance Appraisals* tell the employee if he ended up where he was supposed to in terms of progress toward objectives, day-to-day responsibilities and skill/ability improvements.

- *Goal-setting* concerns "setting the course" for the next year in terms of objectives, responsibilities and skill/abilities which need development.

2. *Coaching* is the step in which you are a mentor. In this part of the cycle, you are keeping the employee on course once the course has been set. You, as the manager, have two goals: (1) to ensure that the employee maintains effective levels of performance and (2) to improve performance when the work gets off course or drops in quality.

Positive Performance Management
Performance Appraisal Overview

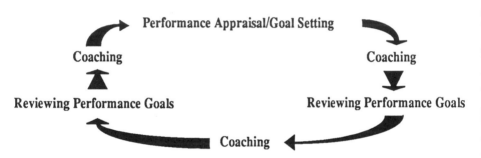

3. *Reviewing Performance Goals* represents an opportunity for the manager and employee to re-examine the goals set earlier in the year. Sometimes the goals set earlier no longer make sense, may have been met or may be unrealistic, so they must be revised. Reviewing performance goals also gives the manager and employee an opportunity to determine if the employee is still on course.

Positive Performance Management is a "checks and balances" system that helps keep employees performing at consistently high levels. While each of the three components are distinct in time, they are not distinct in philosophy or content. *Common to all is the notion of feedback.* Through feedback, employees learn what they are doing well and what they are not doing well. Accordingly, adjustments can be made. Feedback, however, can be a form of recognition and reward. Through rewards, employees associate what they did well with the appropriate reward, causing them to continue performing at high levels.

4

WHAT ARE THE BENEFITS OF POSITIVE PERFORMANCE MANAGEMENT ?

- *It Encourages Communication* — Positive Performance Management emphasizes dialogue between the manager and employee throughout the year. In the Goal-Setting part of the Performance AppraisalGoal-Setting meeting, as well as in the less formal Coaching and Reviewing Performance Goals meetings, you have many opportunities for open, honest dialogue. This is the foundation of effective employee relations.

- *It Is a Tool to Plan, Assess and Control* — Not to control the employee but rather the employee's performance. Any organization's ability to control an employee's performance to the employee's and organization's advantage depends upon how honest and accurate the performance feedback is.

- *It Allows You Re-examination of Organizational and Departmental Objectives* — Positive Performance Management links the objectives and direction of the organization with the specific objectives set for an employee in a given department. It enables employees to work on activities and objectives which are consistent with the organization's objectives. In this way, the task of objective-setting with employees represents a means of implementing short-term strategy within the organization. For those who write action plans, their list of goals or objectives and actions should correlate with the objectives which come from the Performance Appraisal/Goal-Setting meeting.

- *It Is a Means of Planning Compensation* — It should be any organization's philosophy to recognize the strategic link between performance and pay. However, in all cases, the discussion of pay and performance should be separated. By separating the discussion, both the manager and the employee can focus objectively on the performance issues at hand without the pay distraction.

- *It Helps in Career Planning* — Because employees are rated on skills and abilities (how they do their jobs), there exists the opportunity to compare employee skill and ability levels with the standards required for success in higher-level positions. Positive Performance Management can contribute to decisions on the promotability and potential of all employees. It is critical that the organization take the necessary steps to determine the potential of its employees so that appropriate development plans, which are in the best interests of the employee and organization, are acted on.

- *It Helps in Analyzing Training Needs* — The opportunity exists to identify either external or internal training courses which can help develop employees' skills and abilities.

How Does the Manager Benefit?

- *Improved Communications*— Beginning with objective-setting and clarifying expectations and ending with the formal Performance Appraisal/Goal-Setting meeting, you and your employees will have considerable opportunity to be open with each other. This can only lead to open, honest employee relations — the goal of Positive Performance Management.

- *Opportunity to Give Accurate Feedback* — Aside from the more formal once-a-year Performance Appraisal/Goal-Setting meeting, you will have considerable opportunity throughout the year to give positive and constructive feedback to your employees. Feedback given throughout the year (as opposed to once a year) makes giving feedback in the Performance Appraisal/Goal-Setting meeting somewhat easier. Also, your employees should be more accepting of what you have to say because they will have heard how they were doing all year long.

- *Additional Comfort and Control* — So often, managers who are under great stress respond ineffectively to employees who may be the principal contributors to the stress.

    Sometimes, you have to deal with an employee who is not a good performer and/or is a disciplinary case. Many managers attempt to handle this by controlling the person, not the performance — for example, by using threats and imposing very tight schedules on expected performance. Positive Performance Management, if practiced well, will allow you to handle these stressful situations in a more effective way. By controlling performance rather than the person, you are in a better position to justify your personnel decisions — promotion, discipline and termination.

- *Greater Confidence and Better Relations with Your Employees* — Like anything else, the more you practice, the better you get. If you use this approach correctly, you will see your employees performing at consistently high levels with little fluctuation. They will be meeting your expectations, thus contributing to your organization's objectives.

Your employees will see a manager who cares, is positive and appreciates involving his employees in setting goals and assessing performance.

- *Better Performance Appraisals from Your Boss* — Practicing Positive Performance Management should result in a better appraisal from your boss. All managers and supervisors who do performance appraisals should be held accountable for the way they conduct them. All salaried performance appraisal forms, therefore, should contain a measurement factor called "Development of People" (includes coaching, monitoring and performance appraisals.)

How Does the Employee Benefit?

- *You, the Employee, Know What's Expected* — Throughout the year, your manager will have the opportunity to communicate, reinforce and, if necessary, revise what he expects of you. Ideally, your manager will involve you in setting those expectations. In any case, with a clearer idea of what your manager expects, you have a better chance of responding in a way that is consistent with those expectations.

- *You Have Realistic Ideas on Strengths and Weaknesses* — At any point in time, you should know where you stand in the organization. Part of that involves having an accurate profile of your strengths and weaknesses. The opportunity exists in Positive Performance Management for your manager to provide this realistic assessment throughout the year.

- *You Get Recognition* — Throughout the year, your manager will have the opportunity to provide accurate, timely and positive feedback, thereby increasing your expectations that a certain level of effort leads to high levels of performance. This, in turn, results in rewards — which are satisfying to you and are the basis of motivation.

- *You Participate* — Years of behavioral science research has shown that participation, in itself, is rewarding to employees. It satisfies self-esteem needs. Most important, though, participation creates feelings of ownership. This causes you to value and have a positive attitude toward that which is owned (your performance appraisal). Indeed, your manager should involve you in the assessment of your own performance and in objective-setting for the next year.

- *You Get a Better Performance Appraisal from Your Boss* — The best appraisal you can receive is one that is honest, accurate and truly reflective of where you stand. While your manager certainly has responsibility to give you an accurate assessment, it is important to recognize that you can influence the accuracy of your own rating. You must have the right attitude. That is, you need to recognize that feedback is the basis for growth and development and you should assume that your manager has the best intentions. You should also take responsibility for your own appraisal and development (i.e., clarify expectations, seek feedback).

5

HOW DOES A MANAGER CARRY OUT POSITIVE PERFORMANCE MANAGEMENT ?

The major steps in Performance Appraisal/Goal-Setting are preparation, assessment and planning.

Do These Things To Prepare:

1. Schedule

- Plan times when you and your employee can give the subject the proper time and attention.

- Allow no phone calls or other interruptions.

- Sit and face each other either at a table in the office or without a table. (You, the manager, should not use your desk. So often the desk is perceived as a symbol of power and lowers the quality of discussion.)

- Depending on your own comfort level, you may choose to have your meeting on neutral territory — for example, in a conference room.

2. Review Employee's Performance Beforehand

- Determine the extent to which your employee has met the agreed-upon objectives and responsibilities. To do this, it is important that you rely on various indices of your employee's performance (for example, notes kept on file, reports, memos). You should go into the performance appraisal meeting with your notes either penciled in on the performance appraisal form or on note paper.

- Meet with your boss and gather his observations and thoughts about the employee's performance. The discussion should be detailed enough so that you and your boss can agree on a rating. (It is important that you and your boss have a discussion prior to the meeting you have with your employee.)

- It is important to note that while you will enter the meeting with your employee with a rating in mind, it may change depending upon the employee's perception of his performance. Be somewhat flexible.

3. Prepare the Employee

- Present the meeting to your employee as one that will be mutually beneficial.

- Indicate that money will not be discussed, but the rating which results from the meeting will be a factor in determining any salary increase.

- Indicate that performance will be discussed and future goals and plans for meeting those goals will be set.

- Make sure the employee understands that he is expected to come to the meeting prepared to discuss his performance, his skills/abilities which need improvement and the next year's goals.

- Be sure that you give your employee one week to prepare.

- Give your employee a blank copy of the performance appraisal form to organize his own thoughts on his performance and goals for next year. This form does not have to be seen by you. It is a resource for your employee.

4. Judge Yourself

- Consider the possibility that subjective factors are getting in the way of giving your employee a true rating. You should ask yourself if there are any stereotypic attitudes, sexual biases, etc., which may be influencing the rating. ("I can't stand the way he chews gum . . . but he doesn't meet the customers, so what does it matter?") In essence, you want the performance rating to be as close as possible to the theoretical true measure of proficiency. Onc way to achieve this is to ensure that you are rating employees just on factors which determine success in their jobs.

5. Set the Agenda

- Map out the direction in which you want the appraisal meeting to go. "I want to cover this topic, then this topic. Sometime in the early part of the meeting, we need to hit these three points. Then I want to end on this point."

- Open the meeting by stating the objectives and setting a participatory tone.

- Give your employee the opportunity to present his self-assessment first.

- Respond and work with your employee to look for causes of problems and solutions.

- End the meeting by setting objectives and plans for meeting those objectives.

Do These Things to Assess:

1. Share the Agenda

- State the objectives and the agenda.

- Indicate that together you and your employee will determine how well the employee did compared to pre-established objectives and responsibilities.

- Mention that you and your employee also will determine objectives and responsibilities for the next year.

- Emphasize to your employee that he will "carry the ball" in the meeting and that he will present his self-assessment to begin the meeting.

2. *Let the Employee Present His Self-Assessment* — The benefits of allowing an employee to begin with a self-assessment include:

- You avoid putting your employee on the defensive.

- You reinforce in the employee's mind that his involvement is key to the meeting.

- By listening, you learn more about your employee.

- It provides you the opportunity to give negative feedback without ever really giving it. In fact, your employee gives it to himself. Because of this, the employee is in a better position to openly discuss and address his poor performance.

3. *Listen Well and Actively*

- Listen for emotional and logical content.

- Watch facial expressions and mannerisms for clues as to the true meaning of each message.

- If the spoken word appears to contradict facial expressions and mannerisms, make sure you mention it to your employee.

- Summarize key points to ensure he knows you understand his message.

If the person does not open up with his self-assessment, make sure you ask some open-ended questions. (For example, "What do you think about...?")

4. *Respond — the Power of Positive Performance Management*

When responding to your employee, be sure that your employee understands and accepts the message you are trying to communicate. You do not want your employee to be defensive and emotional toward your comments. *You want a "win-win" appraisal.* To get a "win-win" appraisal, you need to be sensitive to what you say, how you say it and when you say it. Listed below are four situations which can occur during a "win-win" appraisal:

- You agree with the employee's positive comments.
- You agree with the employee's negative comments.
- You disagree with the employee's negative comments.
- You disagree with the employee's positive comments.

Patterns to follow when any of the above "agree" or "disagree" situations arise are explained below, step-by-step. Here you will find how to make progress regardless of disagreement or agreement.

Agree/Positive (See Figure 1, Page 20)

- Begin your assessment by mentioning what you agree with that the employee said was positive about himself. The likelihood of anyone becoming defensive in this situation is slim. ("I agree. You have really gotten the group to cooperate with you and with one another.")

- Mention that you agree with your employee's self-perception, thereby rewarding your employee's ability to know himself. ("I see the same big improvement in your communication skills that you do.")

- Mention specific behaviors and their effects, giving support for your agreement. People like to see that you can back-up what you're saying. ("When you asked Bill to give his point of view and then listened to every last word, you showed a new interest and skill.")

- Let your employee know that what he did satisfied your needs. ("That's what I want you to do to help increase quality.")

- Indicate that you appreciate what the employee did. ("It takes effort, doesn't it? I appreciate that.")

- Ask the employee to keep up the good work. ("Keep it up. Let's see some more of it.")

Agree/Negative (See Figure 2, Page 21)

- This is a perfect chance for you to give negative feedback without actually giving it. In fact, your employee gives it to himself. ("Yes, there were some lapses.")

- Mention that you agree with your employee's judgment, thereby rewarding your employee's ability to know himself. ("You show insight when you can pick out your own mistakes.")

- Mention specific behaviors and their effects on your and your department's performance. ("When you forget to listen, I see decreases in morale and often our quality level drops for two days.")

- Address possible causes of the problem. They might be attributable to motivational troubles, skill deficiencies or other factors. Because the employee brought up the negatives, he is more likely to want to discuss the negatives as well as ways to solve them. ("I wonder if you see a subordinate's complaint as a black mark against you. Do you feel attacked when they complain?")

- Identify a plan which can address whatever problem exists. ("Ask the biggest complainers to sit down with you and analyze the origins of the problems.")

Disagree/Negative (See Figure 3, Page 22)

- Bring up the items the employee thought were negative about himself that you disagree with. ("You say you're not well educated. I think you have a good mind for this work. But I do agree you need more experience.")

- State your disagreement. ("I don't think one year in this position teaches everything. You'll be able to learn new things almost every day.")

- Follow with behaviors and statements which lend support to your judgment. ("I know I was still learning when I left the job you're in now.")

- Check with the employee to see if he now agrees with you. If not, loop back and present more behaviors which support your judgment. ("Do you see that? Can you see the growth possibilities? My boss said he was still learning on that job when he had it.")

- If your employee agrees with your judgment, ask him to continue performing in accordance with your judgment.

("I want you to keep looking at this job as a place to learn almost every day.")

Disagree/Positive (See Figure 4, Page 23)

- At this point you have completed 75 percent of your assess ment. If you have followed these steps, it is unlikely that you have caused your employee to become defensive. You have progressed through a good portion of your assessment without providing negative feedback. Indeed, you have set a positive tone for addressing those items which you disagree with that your employee deemed positive about himself. ("You feel you hit all three objectives 90 percent or more. I'd say on number three it is less than that.")

- State your disagreement. ("I gauged your work on the third objective to be both good and poor, sometimes right on target but sometimes not.")

- Mention supporting behaviors and circumstances. ("Remember Nancy asked for June's assignment and you didn't hear her out?")

- Make sure your employee agrees with your judgment; if not, loop back and provide more examples. Once you have agreement, address potential causes of the problems and plans for addressing them. ("Could you have listened another two minutes? Scott wanted your attention. Next time, listen all the way through, okay?")

- Identify certain goals/responsibilities that the employee failed to mention in his self-assessment. ("Did you forget turnover? We wanted that kept under last year's rate.")

- Ask your employee to assess how well he performed these goals/responsibilities and respond accordingly, using the quadrant approach illustrated. ("You say turnover is the same or less. Yes, you worked on it and showed real understanding but didn't get your result. It is still high. Will you work on it this year?")

- Your response is dependent on how positive your employee saw his performance and whether you agree or disagree with his self-assessment.

FIGURE 1

RESPONDING
AGREE/POSITIVE
EMPLOYEE

	POSITIVE	NEGATIVE
AGREE	• State agreement (reward) • Behaviors • Effects on staff, department • Appreciation (need satisfaction) • Keep it up (learning) **"Win-Win"**	
MANAGER		
DISAGREE		

FIGURE 2
RESPONDING AGREE/NEGATIVE EMPLOYEE

POSITIVE ——→ NEGATIVE

	POSITIVE	NEGATIVE
AGREE	• State agreement (reward) • Behaviors • Effects on staff, department • Appreciation (need satisfaction) • Keep it up (learning) "Win-Win"	• State agreement (reward) • Behaviors • Effects on staff, department • What's causing issue? • What can we do to solve? "Win-Win"
MANAGER		
DISAGREE		

FIGURE 3
RESPONDING
DISAGREE/NEGATIVE
EMPLOYEE

POSITIVE —————→ NEGATIVE

	POSITIVE	NEGATIVE
AGREE	• State agreement (reward) • Behaviors • Effects on staff, department • Appreciation (need satisfaction) • Keep it up (learning) **"Win-Win"**	• State agreement (reward) • Behaviors • Effects on staff, department • What's causing issue? • What can we do to solve? **"Win-Win"**
MANAGER		
DISAGREE		• State disagreement (unfreeze) • Behaviors • Effects on staff, department • Check agreement • Keep it up (refreeze) **"Win-Win"**

22

FIGURE 4

RESPONDING
DISAGREE/POSITIVE
EMPLOYEE

	POSITIVE	NEGATIVE
AGREE	• State agreement (reward) • Behaviors • Effects on staff, department • Appreciation (need satisfaction) • Keep it up (learning) "Win-Win"	• State agreement (reward) • Behaviors • Effects on staff, department • What's causing issue? • What can we do to solve? "Win-Win"
DISAGREE	• State disagreement (unfreeze) • Behaviors • Effects on staff, department • Check agreement • What's causing the issue? • What can we do to solve? (unfreeze) "Win-Win"	• State disagreement (unfreeze) • Behaviors • Effects on staff, department • Check agreement • Keep it up (refreeze) "Win-Win"

MANAGER

23

Plan for the Future:

1. Have the Employee Outline His Objectives

- Tell your employee to begin by stating the objectives he has set for himself along with plans for meeting them.

- Indicate that unlike the assessment phase where you, the manager, waited until the employee finished his self-assessment before rendering your assessment, you will respond to each goal, responsibility and skill/ability mentioned by him at the time it comes up. This is because you and your employee must work toward a consensus on each goal, responsibility and skill/ability needing improvement.

- Listen to what the employee is saying.

- Work toward a consensus on each item.

- Check to see if the employee agrees with the goals and responsibilities that have been set.

2. Agree on Goals — When working toward a consensus with your employee, it is important that you base your comments on:

- Department goals.

- The employee's job.

- Strengths and weaknesses of the employee.

- The environment.

- The extent of managerial support which can be provided. ("I will help in any way you ask." "I want to see you handle this alone." "I will tell the others you have all my support.")

Personal comments impede progress. Talk about what is needed to get the job done, not about your personal feelings toward the worker. If you don't like the worker's attitude, ask yourself if that is important. Does it affect anyone else's performance? Does it hurt the worker's own performance? If not, that "bad attitude" may be only the employee's problem and no one else's.

3. *Summarize the Meeting* — At this point you should:

- Summarize your employee's performance by mentioning a couple of positive things the employee did along with a couple of items where the employee fell short, if appropriate. ("You improved on two big jobs. You didn't make much progress on this third one.")

- Summarize key goals and responsibilities for next year. ("Next year we need all three of these goals met, and I'm asking you to take charge on each one.")

- Indicate the rating you have given your employee and mention that his observations and comments contributed to this rating. ("My rating of this past year's work is a seven on a scale of zero to ten. I used your evaluations to help me. Thanks for your help.")

- Mention the next steps:
  - You will be filling out the Performance Appraisal form based on the joint discussion.
  - You'll be getting the employee's signature, if appropriate (depends on the organization.)
  - You'll be getting your manager's signature.

It may be appropriate to set another meeting. This depends on the rating. If the employee received a low rating, it is critical that you and your employee agree on short-term objectives and also agree to meet frequently enough to ensure that adequate progress is being made. In all cases, however, thank your employee for his involvement and input and ask if there is anything you can do to help him meet his goals and responsibilities.

4. *Your Additional Responsibilities*

- When there has been a change in employee performance ... If you believe that the employee's performance has changed subsequent to a Performance AppraisalGoal-Setting meeting and prior to your employee's scheduled salary review, complete an up-to-date Performance Appraisal form and review it with your employee.

- Managerial job change . . .
  - If you leave your job due to a transfer, promotion, termination or any other reason
  - Complete your Performance Appraisal meetings and your Performance Appraisal and Goal-Setting Records on those employees who haven't received appraisals in six months or longer.
  - Review the completed appraisals with your replacement.
  - Your replacement should use this appraisal information as either input to the next round of appraisals he will conduct or as the basis for an employee's scheduled merit increase, whichever is appropriate.

6

THE EMPLOYEE'S ROLE IN IMPLEMENTING PPM

What You Need To Do When You Are Getting A Performance Appraisal

The major steps in Performance AppraisalGoal-Setting are: *Preparation, Assessment and Planning*.

How to Prepare:

1. Schedule the Meeting

- Schedule it for a day when you and your manager both can give full attention to the subject.

- Conduct the meeting where you and your manager can have privacy and an interruption-free environment.

2. Know How Your Manager Assesses Your Performance

- Your manager should determine the extent to which you

have met agreed-upon objectives and responsibilities. In doing this, your manager should rely on records of your performance (for example, notes kept on file, reports). Your manager should meet with his manager to review your performance prior to sitting down with you.

3. *Know Your Department's Goals, Objectives and Plans*

- You and your manager should know the department's objectives so that goals can be set. Be sure you are as up-to-date on these objectives as you can be; let your boss lead the way in discussing them, however.

4. *Prepare*

- Review your strengths and weaknesses.

- Predict what your manager might say and be aware of discrepancies between what your manager says and what you think. Be prepared to bring these subjects up *without emotion*. It is possible to disagree agreeably.

- Rehearse your responses to anticipated feedback. *Criticism is not a personal attack*, so don't respond to it that way.

- Recognize that you need feedback to grow, that you are no less a person for accepting guidance. You have the right to choose whether to change as a result of the feedback. If you fail to encourage feedback, you lose the choice and the control that comes with having alternative ways of behaving.

- Assume the best intentions — view the appraiser as a person who wants to give you useful information and wants to help you grow.
  - Avoid going into the discussion with a "loaded gun." If you *expect* that the appraiser will be trying to harm you, it will affect how you hear even the most neutral message.
  - Even if your assumption of good intentions is wrong, responding as if the appraiser is trying to help you can defray a destructive attack.

- Your manager should assume some of the responsibility for helping you prepare for the meeting.

- Your manager should present the meeting as a mutually beneficial discussion.

- While money should not be discussed, your manager should indicate that the rating which results from the meeting will be a factor in determining any salary increase (when you are due).

- Your manager should mention that your performance will be discussed and future goals and plans for meeting those goals will be set.

- Your manager should give you one week to prepare. He may also give you a blank copy of the Performance Appraisal form. You may find this form useful in organizing your thoughts on the past year's performance and goals for next year. This is your tool; you need not give your manager a copy.

5. *Judge Yourself*

- Be clear in your mind about what you've truly contributed in the past year.

6. *Set an Agenda*

- Your manager should map out in his mind before the meeting the direction in which he wants the meeting to go. If he hasn't, be ready to suggest some points to discuss. But, it is his right to guide the conversation — be in a mood to listen.

How to Assess:

1. *Share the Agenda*

- Your manager should begin the meeting by stating the objectives and the agenda.

- Your manager should mention that you will have an equal role in determining how well you performed this year.

- Also, you will play an equal role in setting objectives and responsibilities to guide your future performance.

2. *You Present Your Self-Assessment*

- Your manager will expect you to share with him how well you thought you performed this year.

- Your manager will want you to begin the meeting with your self-assessment.

3. *Listening*

- Your manager should allow you to finish your self-assessment before giving his own assessment. He should listen to what you have to say, interrupting only to make sure he understands your message.

4. *Respond When You Have Listened*

- Once you have completed your self-assessment, it will be your manager's turn to give his assessment. In this regard, your manager should be sensitive to what you say, how you say it and when you say it. This should result in an appraisal that makes you and your manager feel good.

- Regarding your behavior during the discussion — if the feedback is too general, ask for specifics. Ask about specific examples of what the appraiser is saying.

- Find out if feedback is based on one incident or several and if a pattern seems to exist.

- For negative criticism, work with your manager in determining more acceptable behavior.

- If no positive feedback occurs, ask for examples of things the manager likes. If only positive feedback is given, ask for areas which need improvement. Avoid acting defensively and make it clear to the manager that he is being heard.

- Use re-statements (re-state what your manager has said in your own words).

- Use open body language (forward lean, eye contact, arms and legs uncrossed).

How to Plan:
1. Present Your Ideas

- Your manager should ask you to present the goals you have set for yourself along with plans for meeting them.

- Your manager should ask you to present each goal, responsibility and skill/ability needing development one at a time.

2. Listen

- Your manager should respond and work with you to reach agreement on goals and responsibilities. This represents the beginning of taking responsibility for your performance and your ultimate appraisal.

- By all means clarify your manager's expectations early.

3. Continually Check on Your Progress

- As the year unfolds, ask for feedback — the more you ask, the more skilled you become in receiving it and the better off you are.

7

THE MANAGER'S ROLE IN IMPLEMENTING THE "COACHING" COMPONENT OF PPM

Coaching is an integral part of a manager's daily job. It consists of: (1) maintaining effective performance and, (2) improving employee performance. In Goal-Setting, a course is set for the year. In Coaching, the activities are aimed at ensuring that your employee stays on course. Coaching is part of the mentoring process; you need to establish a relationship with your employee based on mutual respect and trust.

The Major Steps in Maintaining Effective Performance:

1. Describe Effective Performance

- Reward your employee in a way that will encourage him to continue performing at that level.

- In timing your rewards, it is best if your employee is unable to predict the time at which he will be rewarded. That is,

use an intermittent schedule when giving an employee
certain rewards.

* Let your employee know the specific performance with
  which you are pleased.

* Be *specific* and *sincere.*

2. Tell the Importance of Effective Performance

* Let your employee know that his performance is highly
  valued and that what he has accomplished has had a
  positive impact on your performance and that of others in
  the department.

* Be specific when pointing out these positive effects. This
  type of feedback enhances your employee's self-esteem
  and will encourage him to maintain that effective level of
  performance.

3. Listen

* Listen empathetically to your employee's comments.

* Make sure you summarize your employee's key points and
  say them back to him to ensure he knows you understand
  his message.

4. Volunteer Your Continued Help

* Show your commitment to maintaining your employee's
  high level performance by asking him if there is anything
  you can do to make it easier for him to do his job.

5. Indicate Your Intention to Take Action

* If your employee needs your help, by all means say that
  you will take action to get help for him.

6. Thank the Employee

* A sincere "thank you" on your part goes a long way,
  encouraging your employee to continue his good
  performance because it's appreciated.

8

THE MAJOR STEPS IN IMPROVING EMPLOYEE PERFORMANCE

1. Describe the Problem in a Friendly Manner

- You, as the manager, must address the matter when an employee's performance needs improvement.

- Handle the discussion with your employee in such a way that he is motivated to improve performance.

- Begin by describing the problem in a friendly manner.

- Point out specific behaviors which you have observed that support your judgment.

2. Ask the Employee for Help

- Discuss the causes. Have your employee focus on the performance problem. Many times your employee will avoid discussing the actual problem. Try to listen and ask repeatedly to get the problem out in the open.

- Search for causes. The reasons for not meeting standards could be many. They could be caused by skill or motivational problems.

3. Identify and Write Down Solutions

- Involve your employee in developing solutions.

- If your employee comes up with a solution, try to use his idea. This has a positive influence on your employee's motivation.

4. Decide on Specific Actions to Take

- You and your employee should decide the specific actions each of you should take. The actions you may take could include providing extra resources to your employee or making yourself more accessible.

- Communicate to your employee that his effective performance is so meaningful to you that you're willing to take the steps and time necessary to help him be a success.

5. Agree on Specific Follow-Up Dates

- Good plans are realistic, challenging and time-limited.

- Your employee needs to know when improved performance is expected.

9

YOUR ROLE AS MANAGER IN REVIEWING PERFORMANCE GOALS

You and your employee should review the goals that were set at the Performance Appraisal/Goal-Setting meeting or at some other point in the year. Goals set but not reviewed are not all that worthwhile.

In this discussion, emphasis is placed on your employee reporting his progress-to-date toward goals. You and your employee also need to focus on deviations and progress-to-date indications that goals either will be exceeded or not met. If your employee is on a pace that will exceed the goal, you and your employee should discuss how added effort and/or resources could make performance exceed the goal. Many times, supervisors ignore performance that is above the goal and spend too much time on performance that is below the goal.

If your employee is on a course that is below goal, you and he should discuss causes, examine solutions and agree on appropriate actions. In some cases you may consider adjusting the goal downward. The review session may bring out additional objectives which are important now but were not at the time the original "contract" was set.

The Major Steps in Reviewing Goals:

1. Ask the Employee to Meet for a Review Session; Have the Employee Estimate Progress-to-Date

- Begin your meeting by asking your employee to estimate progress-to-date toward each goal.

- Listen to your employee's comments and take notes.

2. Discuss Progress and Praise Your Employee

- You and your employee need to engage in fact-finding and determining progress-to-date.

- It is vital that regardless of how far away your employee is from meeting the goal, you praise him for his progress-to-date.

3. Re-Negotiate Goals and/or Resources Where Deviation Is Significant

- Focus on deviations.

- If the deviation is downward, you and your employee should discuss causes and solutions to agree on appropriate actions. Appropriate actions may include increasing available resources, agreeing on activities which will enable your employee to meet goals or adjust the goals downward.

- If, on the other hand, your employee is exceeding goals, you should discuss how added effort and/or resources may be utilized to further exceed the goal. You and your employee may decide to add additional goals at this time as well.

4. Write Down New Agreements and Set a Follow-Up Date

- Take notes during the discussion. These should be used as a summary of the agreements so that both you and your employee can review them.

- A new follow-up session should be scheduled at a time when the data will be available to evaluate progress toward the goal(s).

- Thank your employee.

THE ROLE OF HUMAN RESOURCE / PERSONNEL DEPARTMENTS IN PPM

While Positive Performance Management serves as a "checks and balances" system to help keep employees performing consistently at high levels, the real effectiveness of Positive Performance Management is only achieved when your company provides a "checks and balances" on the system itself. In other words, Positive Performance Management can only be effective when your company "manages" the system from start-up to implementation to ensure it is, in fact, doing what it's capable of doing.

Usually, the one department given responsibility for the role of "managing" the performance review system is the Human Resource/Personnel Department. In that role, most Human Resource/Personnel Departments take the necessary steps to ensure that: review forms/instructions are distributed on time, review forms are completed and that the forms are filed properly. While all of this is often administratively and legally acceptable, it often comes across to everyone as a slow, mechanical, boring and bureaucratic paper exercise that benefits no one. In effect, an administratively *conceived* performance review system leads to an administratively *perceived* system which, in fact, serves no benefit.

Therefore, Human Resource/Personnel Departments should take the necessary steps to develop a more comprehensive and, thus, a more meaningful role when it comes to "managing" performance review systems. For example, in implementing Positive Performance Management or any similar performance review system, there are three separate and distinct roles for the Personnel Department:

- Educative

- Facilitative

- Evaluative

The educative role is a step prior to the actual performance review process. It involves all of those steps a Personnel Department should take to ensure that managers and employees have the knowledge and skills needed to conduct honest, accurate reviews.

The facilitative role is a transition step requiring action, involvement and proactivity on the part of the Personnel Department. It involves those steps this department should take to ensure they are seen as advisors and consultants to managers and employees.

The evaluative role is a post-review step involving research and critiques by the Personnel Department aimed at determining whether the performance review system is, in fact, doing what it's capable of.

Also, for each role there are corresponding "success factors" that should be considered in measuring how well your Personnel Department is "managing" the system. Listed below you will find a handy checklist of criteria for each role.

Real success in achieving honest, accurate reviews which simultaneously meet the needs of your managers and employees depends on how well your company meets these standards. As you implement PPM, it is vital that you continually evaluate and adjust your system when necessary.

Criteria for the Educative Role *(circle one)*	Strongly Disagree	Disagree	Agree	Strongly Agree

Research Activities

1. The forms were developed with employee/ manager input.   SD D A SA

2. The process of performance appraisal was developed with employee/manager input.   SD D A SA

3. The forms and process were developed after reviewing performance appraisal systems in other excellent companies.   SD D A SA

4. The forms and process reflect the company's goals, culture and traditions.   SD D A SA

Design Activities

1. The forms are valid; that is, they measure what they are supposed to measure.   SD D A SA

2. The forms are reliable; that is, they facilitate consistent, stable ratings over time.   SD D A SA

3. The forms are readable, understandable and practical.   SD D A SA

4. Managers are held accountable for the information they place on the forms.   SD D A SA

5. Employees can acknowledge that they had a performance appraisal goal-setting discussion on the form itself.   SD D A SA

6. Employees can write down their comments about the performance appraisal session on the form itself.   SD D A SA

7. The forms measure employee's progress toward agreed-upon objectives.   SD D A SA

8. The forms measure the progress of the employee toward agreed-upon responsibilities.   SD D A SA

9. The forms measure how results were accomplished.   SD D A SA

	Strongly Disagree	Disagree	Agree	Strongly Agree
10. The forms accommodate new objectives and plans for meeting them.	SD	D	A	SA
11. The forms accommodate new responsibilities and plans for meeting them.	SD	D	A	SA
12. The forms accommodate the identification of skills/abilities which need development along with plans for improvement.	SD	D	A	SA
13. The final rating reflects how well the employee has progressed against agreed-upon objectives, responsibilities and skill/ability levels required for success.	SD	D	A	SA
14. The forms have accompanying instructions which detail how the forms should be filled out.	SD	D	A	SA
15. The performance management system at this company is designed to be more than a once-a year meeting between managers and employees.	SD	D	A	SA
16. The performance management system relies heavily on employee involvement.	SD	D	A	SA
17. The performance management system is designed to result in "win-win" interactions between managers and employees.	SD	D	A	SA
18. Performance appraisal/discussions are designed to be separate from salary discussions.	SD	D	A	SA
19. The performance management system relies heavily on manager employee preparation.	SD	D	A	SA

Education Activities

1. Managers are well trained in the proper use of the forms.	SD	D	A	SA
2. Managers are well trained in the process i.e., what to say, how to say it, when to say it.	SD	D	A	SA

	Strongly Disagree	Disagree	Agree	Strongly Agree
3. Employees are well trained in the proper use of the forms.	SD	D	A	SA
4. Employees are informed about the process of performance appraisal.	SD	D	A	SA
5. Trainers are well prepared and trained to conduct performance appraisal training in their locations.	SD	D	A	SA
6. Instructor manuals are comprehensive, clear and complete.	SD	D	A	SA
7. Participant workbooks are comprehensive, clear and complete.	SD	D	A	SA

Administrative Activities

1. Employees receive their performance appraisals on time.	SD	D	A	SA
2. Forms and instructions are disseminated to managers on time.	SD	D	A	SA
3. Performance appraisal training is done on time.	SD	D	A	SA

Marketing Activities

1. Senior management understands and is committed to the performance management system.	SD	D	A	SA
2. Middle management understands and is committed to the performance management system.	SD	D	A	SA
3. Supervisors understand and are committed to the system.	SD	D	A	SA
4. Employees understand and are committed to the system	SD	D	A	SA

Criteria for the Facilitative Role (*circle one*) *Diagnostic Activities Following Interview*	Strongly Disagree	Disagree	Agree	Strongly Agree
1. The forms are complete.	SD	D	A	SA
2. The forms include the necessary signatures.	SD	D	A	SA
3. The final rating reflects how well employees have progressed with agreed-upon objectives, responsibilities and skill/ability levels required for success.	SD	D	A	SA
4. New goals and plans for meeting them appear on the form.	SD	D	A	SA
5. New responsibilities and plans for meeting them appear on the form.	SD	D	A	SA
6. Skills/abilities which need development and performance improvement plans appear on the form.	SD	D	A	SA
7. Each completed form is thoroughly read and reviewed in the Personnel Department before it is filed.	SD	D	A	SA
8. All written comments are legal.	SD	D	A	SA

Assessment Activities

1. Throughout the performance appraisal process, the Personnel Department actively seeks feedback from employees/managers on how well the process is going.	SD	D	A	SA

Consultative Activities

1. Personnel Department "coaches" employees/ managers on how to prepare for performance appraisal sessions.	SD	D	A	SA
2. Personnel Department "coaches" employees/ managers on how to handle the actual appraisal discussion, providing direction and guidance as needed.	SD	D	A	SA
3. Personnel Department representatives are a resource in the actual discussion, providing direction and guidance as needed.	SD	D	A	SA

	Strongly Disagree	Disagree	Agree	Strongly Agree
4. Personnel Department responds appropriately to employee claims of mistreatment, unfairness and strong disagreement with the rating.	SD	D	A	SA
5. Personnel Department provides support and guidance to managers/employees in disciplinary situations.	SD	D	A	SA
6. Where performance is less than good, the comments support the rating and clearly communicate the problems.	SD	D	A	SA
7. Where performance is less than good, the Personnel Department has met with both parties to ensure there is accurate communication about expectations.	SD	D	A	SA
8. Where performance is less than good, a specific performance improvement plan has been agreed to.	SD	D	A	SA
9. Where performance is less than good, a specific "less than normal" time framework has been established to review progress.	SD	D	A	SA

Criteria for the Evaluative Role *(circle one)*

Evaluation Activities

	Strongly Disagree	Disagree	Agree	Strongly Agree
1. The forms are seen as valid and reliable.	SD	D	A	SA
2. The process of performance appraisal is seen as fair and honest.	SD	D	A	SA
3. Managers and employees perceive that pay is contingent on performance.	SD	D	A	SA
4. Managers and employees perceive a link between the types of training certain employees receive and their skill/ability levels.	SD	D	A	SA
5. Through Personnel Department research, there are improved "success rates" of those promoted into higher positions with the help of the performance appraisal system.	SD	D	A	SA
6. Through Personnel Department research, the Company can better justify (using performance appraisals) the discipline and termination decisions that are made.	SD	D	A	SA
7. Through Personnel Department research, managers and employees pursue training activities consistent with the results of their appraisals.	SD	D	A	SA
8. Performance appraisals are seen as more than a once-a-year process.	SD	D	A	SA
9. Employee involvement is practiced actively in the performance appraisal process.	SD	D	A	SA
10. Performance appraisals are seen as "win-win" interactions between managers and employees.	SD	D	A	SA
11. Performance appraisal discussions are, in fact, separate from salary discussions.	SD	D	A	SA
12. Managers/employees do, in fact, adequately prepare themselves for the performance appraisal discussion.	SD	D	A	SA
13. Managers feel they are accountable for the information they place on the form.	SD	D	A	SA

APPENDIX B

PERFORMANCE APPRAISAL AND GOAL-SETTING RECORD

The Performance Appraisal and Goal-Setting Record consists of two parts: (1) Performance Appraisal and (2) Goal-Setting. Performance Appraisals rate how well your employees performed against pre-established work objectives and handled day-to-day responsibilities. Furthermore, it measures the manner in which your employees' accomplishments were achieved. Goal-Setting, on the other hand, allows you to record agreed-upon objectives, day-to-day responsibilities and specific plans for your employees' improvement.

Performance Appraisal

Accomplishment of Major Work Objectives

In this section, record in priority order major work objectives which you set with your employee in last year's performance appraisal session. If there were additional objectives and/or any changes to agreed-upon objectives throughout the year, however, be sure to record all such additions and the most recent revisions to any objective. Moreover, space is provided for you to record specific results achieved by your employee against those objectives. It is important in recording these results to include only factual information regarding how and when results were achieved. For some non-supervisory employees, this section may not apply. If this is the case, write "NA" in this section.

Accomplishment of Day-to-Day Work Responsibilities

In this section, record in priority order day-to-day work responsibilities and specific results achieved. To record responsibilities, it is always helpful to go to your employee's job description (i.e., if one exists) and extract those responsibilities that you consider critical. The best place to look, however, should be your employee's performance appraisal form completed the previous year. One of the products of an effective performance appraisal/goal-setting session is agreement between yourself and your employee on what constitutes major, ongoing work responsibilities. You will find that in the Goal-Setting section of the Record, space is provided to accommodate mutually agreed-upon responsibilities. In recording results against responsibilities, however, it is important that you indicate actual behavioral observations you made throughout the year in support of your assessment.

Other Significant Accomplishments

Many times an employee goes beyond the "call of duty" and contributes to the Company in areas and ways which were not mutually agreed-upon objectives and/or responsibilities. For example, the employee who on his own initiative becomes a member of an interdepartment task team or who establishes a reputation for excellence with associates, managers and customers who are not ordinary contacts. The employees who do produce these results have a habit of translating initiative and effort into results, productivity and success. Accordingly, when filling in this section, you should record specific behaviors and incidents which lend support to your assessment.

How Results Were Accomplished

In this section, for each skill and ability: (1) place an "X" in the box that best represents the level of employee skill/ability compared with your perception of the level required for successful job performance and (2) provide specific examples that support your rating. The rationale is that an employee's performance rating depends on what was accomplished as well as how it was accomplished. This section also provides a springboard for identifying specific employee development needs as they relate to "successful" performance in that given job. Looking to the future, accurate assessments of skill/ability levels provide the basis for estimating the potential of employees by comparing current skill levels with those required for success in higher level jobs. In sum, this section can be used for career development purposes as well.

Overall Performance Rating

Looking back on your employee's performance year, assuming that s/he was working against pre-established and mutually agreed-upon objectives and responsibilities, implies that you can assess the degree to which these standards were met. Adding to the complexity of giving your employee a summary-type rating is the fact that you must also assess your employee's skill/ability level compared with the level required for success in that job.

To aid you in tracking and anchoring your employee's progress toward objectives, responsibilities and required skill/ability levels, a 5-point scale is provided. It ranges from marginal, which is reserved for employees who fail to meet standards or meet them only in part, to outstanding, which is reserved for employees who far exceed the standards of the position. This scale ensures that you base your rating on the performance data you have already covered. Ideally, your summary rating will be consistent with the comments provided in the previous sections of the Record.

While this scale does provide some help to you in tracking your employee's performance, it should be noted that the task is still very much subjective.

Major Work Objectives and/or Work Responsibilities for Next Year

Results from your review meeting with your employee should be the identification of prioritized work objectives and/or responsibilities along with plans for meeting those objectives/responsibilities. In this section, please record those results. For some non-supervisory employees, this section may not apply. If this is the case, write "NA" in this section.

Specific objectives should be challenging but attainable, profitable for the company, within the employee's ability to achieve and mutually understood by you and the employee.

Plans for Performance Improvement

In this section, you should list: (1) specific skills and abilities from the How Results Were Accomplished section of the form that need development and (2) strategies for meeting those development needs.

Ideally, as a result of the meeting, you and the employee will have reached agreement on those skills needing development and discussed how they will be developed. Regarding the latter, you and the employee should consider in-house or external training programs as potential plans. You should also look to re-structuring the employee's work in such a way that allows him/her to gain exposure in areas that need development. For example, an employee who needs to develop verbal communication skills can be provided opportunities to practice that skill.

While filling out the appropriate sections of the Performance Appraisal and Goal-Setting Record, you may find that additional space is required to write down your comments. You may add additional pages, as needed, to accommodate these comments.

Sample:

Performance Appraisal and Goal-Setting Record

Name: _____

Date of this Appraisal: _____

Position: _____

Employment Date: _____

Dept. Division: _____

Date Appointed to Present Job: _____

Performance Appraisal

Accomplishment of Major Work Objectives
List below: (1) major work objectives set last year and (2) specific results against those objectives.

Objectives	Results
1._____	1. _____
	_____
2._____	2. _____
	_____
3._____	3. _____
	_____

Accomplishment of Day-to-Day Work Responsibilities
List below: (1) continuing job responsibilities and (2) results achieved.

Responsibilities	Results
1._____	1. _____
2._____	2. _____
3._____	3. _____

Other Significant Accomplishments (if applicable)
Describe other significant accomplishments which were not (1) major work objectives and/or (2) day-to-day responsibilities.

_____

_____

_____

How Results Were Accomplished — Skill/Ability Levels

For each skill and ability listed below: (1) place an "X" in the box that best represents the level of employee skill/ability compared with the level required for successful job performance and (2) provide specific examples that support your rating. Write in "NA" if not applicable.

Factors	Rating Against Job Requirements			Examples
	Needs Improvement	Met	Exceeded	
1. Judgment and Decision Making — Identifies/evaluates issues; reaches sound conclusions; generates alternatives; understands consequences; makes accurate and timely decisions; attends to details				
2. Drive and Commitment — Maintains high energy level; tackles tough assignments; strives for personal improvement and success				
3. Leadership and Impact — Guides others to work toward common objectives; commands respect; develops cooperation and teamwork; bias toward action				
4. Initiative and Risk-Taking — Self-starting; creative; searches for new ideas; takes calculated risks; sense of urgency about next step				
5. Planning and Resource Management — Forecasts needs; sets priorities; effectively uses financial and human resources; proactive				

Factors	Rating Against Job Requirements			Examples
	Needs Improvement	Met	Exceeded	
6. Interpersonal Skills — Earns acceptance at all levels; establishes and maintains effective relations with relevant individuals and groups				
7. Communication Skills — Presents information verbally and in written form that is clear, concise and accurate; keeps subordinates, associates and supervisors informed; listens				
8. Adaptability — Adjusts practices in changing environment; adapts to new people, ideas and procedures; searches for self-responsibility				
9. Development of People — Sets performance goals; appraises in timely, accurate manner; effective at coaching, mentoring and development planning				
10. Professional Competence and Knowledge — Technically competent in job; knowledge about strategic direction of Company and own department; understands culture				

Overall Performance Rating

Place an "X" in the space that best represents the degree to which the employee met: (a) objectives, (b) work responsibilities and (c) skill/ability levels required for success in his/her current position.

a	b	c	
			Marginal: Fails to meet standards or meets them only in part. Performance is definitely below expectancy.
			Satisfactory: Performance is close to being good, but the need for further improvement is indicated. If performance is below standard in some portions of the responsibility, it is not too far out of line. This rating should have a slightly negative connotation. Need for further development in the case of employees with minimum experience is recognizable.
			Good/Fully Competent: Meets practically all the standards of the position in a completely satisfactory way with a number of instances of above-standard performance. This means that the performance on the whole averages out to what is expected of a seasoned employee.
			Excellent: Meets all standards established for the position and in many instances exceeds them. This represents a seasoned employee's superior performance which is clearly better than good.
			Outstanding: In general, far exceeds the standards of this position; operates in all areas at top performance. This rating is not to be regarded as an absolute superlative or a degree of perfection which is impossible to obtain; rather it is a rating reserved for those whose outstanding performance is clearly obvious to all.

Goal-Setting

Major Work Objectives and/or Responsibilities for Next Year
List below: (1) major work objectives and/or work responsibilities for next year and (2) plans for meeting those objectives and/or responsibilities. Indicate objectives with an "O" and responsibilities with an "R."

Objectives/Responsibilities   Plans

1. _____   1. _____

2. _____   2. _____

3. _____   3. _____

4. _____   4. _____

5. _____   5. _____

Plans for Performance Improvement
List below: (1) specific skills and abilities from the "How Results Were Accomplished" section of the form that need to be developed and (2) plans for meeting those development needs.

Development Area   Plans

1. _____   1. _____
   _____   _____

2. _____   2. _____
   _____   _____

3. _____   3. _____
   _____   _____

_____   _____
                Appraised by   Date

_____   _____
        Appraiser's manager's concurrence   Date

I participated in a Performance Appraisal and Goal-Setting Discussion with my supervisor. Further, I have read the content recorded in this Performance Appraisal and Goal-Setting Record. My comments are as follows:

_____   _____
            Employee's Signature   Date

INDEX

Buy two, get one free!

Each of our handbook series (LIFESTYLE, COMMUNICATION, PRODUCTIVITY and LEADERSHIP) was designed to give you the most comprehensive collection of hands-on desktop references all related to a specific topic. They're a great value at the regular price of $12.95 ($14.95 in Canada); plus, at the unbeatable offer of buy two at the regular price and get one free, you can't find a better value in learning resources. **To order**, see the back of this page for the entire handbook selection.

1. Fill out and send the entire page by mail to:

<table>
<tr><td>In U.S.A.:
National Press Publications
6901 West 63rd Street
P.O. Box 2949
Shawnee Mission, Kansas 66201-1349</td><td>In Canada:
National Press Publications
1243 Islington Avenue, Suite 900
Toronto, Ontario M8X 1Y9</td></tr>
</table>

2. Or **FAX 1-913-432-0824**

3. Or call toll-free **1-800-258-7246**

Fill out completely:

Name _____

Organization _____

Address _____

City _____

State/Province _____ Zip/Postal Code _____

Telephone ( ) _____

Method of Payment:

☐ Enclosed is my check or money order

☐ Please charge to:

    ☐ Mastercard   ☐ Visa   ☐ American Express

Signature _____ Exp. Date _____

Credit Card Number

☐☐☐☐☐☐☐☐☐☐☐☐☐☐☐☐

To order multiple copies for coworkers and friends:	U.S.	Can.
20-50 copies	$8.50	$10.95
More than 50 copies	$7.50	$ 9.95

VIP# 705-08458-092

OTHER DESKTOP HANDBOOKS

	Qty	Item #	Title	U.S.	Can.	Total
LEADERSHIP		410	The Supervisor's Handbook, Revised and Expanded	$12.95	$14.95	
		458	Positive Performance Management: *A Guide to Win-Win Reviews*	$12.95	$14.95	
		459	Techniques of Successful Delegation	$12.95	$14.95	
		463	Powerful Leadership Skills for Women	$12.95	$14.95	
		494	Team-Building	$12.95	$14.95	
		495	How to Manage Conflict	$12.95	$14.95	
		469	Peak Performance	$12.95	$14.95	
COMMUNICATION		413	Dynamic Communication Skills for Women	$12.95	$14.95	
		414	The Write Stuff: *A Style Manual for Effective Business Writing*	$12.95	$14.95	
		417	Listen Up: *Hear What's Really Being Said*	$12.95	$14.95	
		442	Assertiveness: *Get What You Want Without Being Pushy*	$12.95 $12.95	$14.95 $14.95	
		460	Techniques to Improve Your Writing Skills	$12.95	$14.95	
		461	Powerful Presentation Skills	$12.95	$14.95	
		482	Techniques of Effective Telephone Communication	$12.95	$14.95	
		485	Personal Negotiating Skills	$12.95	$14.95	
		488	Customer Service: *The Key to Winning Lifetime Customers*	$12.95	$14.95	
		498	How to Manage Your Boss	$12.95	$14.95	
PRODUCTIVITY		411	Getting Things Done: *An Achiever's Guide to Time Management*	$12.95	$14.95	
		443	A New Attitude	$12.95	$14.95	
		468	Understanding the Bottom Line: *Finance for the Non-financial Manager*	$12.95	$14.95	
		483	Successful Sales Strategies: *A Woman's Perspective*	$12.95	$14.95	
		489	Doing Business Over the Phone: *Telemarketing for the '90s*	$12.95	$14.95	
		496	Motivation & Goal-Setting: *The Keys to Achieving Success*	$12.95	$14.95	
LIFESTYLE		415	Balancing Career & Family: *Overcoming the Superwoman Syndrome*	$12.95	$14.95	
		416	Real Men Don't Vacuum	$12.95	$14.95	
		464	Self-Esteem: *The Power to Be Your Best*	$12.95	$14.95	
		484	The Stress Management Handbook	$12.95	$14.95	
		486	Parenting: *Ward & June Don't Live Here Anymore*	$12.95	$14.95	
		487	How to Get the Job You Want	$12.95	$14.95	

SALES TAX All purchases subject to state and local sales tax. Questions? Call 1-800-258-7246.		
Subtotal		
Sales Tax (Add appropriate state and local tax)		
Shipping & Handling ($1 one item, 50¢ each add.)		
Total		

VIP# 705-08458-092